KIDS'
Answers to Life's Big Questions

Steve & Ruth Bennett

Bob Adams, Inc.

Published by Bob Adams, Inc.
260 Center Street, Holbrook, Massachusetts 02343

ISBN: 1-55850-149-5

Printed in Korea

A   B   C   D   E   F   G   H   I   J

COVER ART: Caitlin Marshall (people) and
              Anna Norcross (flowers)

Acknowledgments

First and foremost, we'd like to thank all of the children who took time out of their busy lives and participated in our survey. Those whose answers and drawings were used are listed in the back of the book, in the order in which their contributions appear.

Several other people were key players in this project. Stacey Miller arranged numerous interviews for us. Lisa Fisher, Nancy McGovern, Mary Hanley, and Andrea Dykens did the same. Nancy Lord, Bonnie Seigal, Holt Massey, and Bob Kalish not only interviewed their own children, but helped locate willing participants as well. Jennifer Stoffel, publisher of Cleveland Parenting, conducted numerous interviews for us and gave us entrees to the midwest parent community. Betty Burkes was kind enough to interview her students at the Paradise School in Wellfleet, Massachusetts.

Debbie Milligan collected a treasury of children's artwork for us. Lynn Loetterle passed out surveys at her Alexandria, Virginia store, Definitely Dinosaurs (a great kids' place), while Mary Esther Fournier, pharmacist of Huron Drugs in Cambridge, Massachusetts, had the brainstorm of including interview solicitations as "bag stuffers." Julia Harding of Henry Bear's Park in Cambridge placed the announcements in prominent places, too. Rachel Orefice enabled us to contact children at Lesley Ellis School in Arlington, Massachusetts, and Reverend Lucinda Duncan made it possible for us to interview at the First Parish Church in Cambridge.

David and Emily Hawkins, both experts on talking to children, helped us phrase the questions just right. You were right, folks—very subtle nuances do make all the difference in getting a splendid answer and a blank stare.

Special thanks go to Mike Snell, who also helped us frame the questions—we knew you were fluent in many tongues, friend, but we didn't realize you knew "kidspeak" so well.

Once again, our editor, Brandon Toropov, worked with us as co-conspirator—thanks for the old eagle eye and good thoughts. And we owe Bob Adams our gratitude for supporting the project (it was Bob's stroke of genius to include the artwork).

Finally, we are indebted to our children, Noah and Audrey, for putting up with us while we poured through the surveys and assembled the book. Thanks kids—we owe you about 64,000 walks in the meadow.

Introduction

"Stop work, go outside, and take a long walk in a meadow," our four-year-old son, Noah, suggested in the middle of a hectic work week. We took his advice, and during our walk we began wondering what advice other kids offered their parents for leading happier lives. This evolved into a broader survey designed to find out what four-, five-, and six-year-olds had to say about the meaning of life, liberty, and the pursuit of happiness. After kid-testing our questions locally, we asked parents from Massachusetts to California to share the survey with their children. This book offers a selection of the more than 6,000 answers we received, along with original artwork inspired by the survey topics.

Some of the answers you'll read in the following pages are whimsical or endearing for their naïveté. But you'll also find nuggets of wisdom that put into perspective our own attempts to solve the riddles of everyday life and the world about us. After all, young children are free of the filters and blinders that we, as adults, have acquired through years of school, work, and day-to-day living. And young children aren't so concerned about drawing lines between the actual and the possible—or separating reality from fantasy.

When we see the world through the eyes of our children, we experience what the ancient Zen philosophers called the "untrammeled spirit." We see the world anew, unfettered by judgments and preconceptions. And best of all, we rejuvenate the child within ourselves.

Steve Bennett & Ruth Loetterle Bennett
CAMBRIDGE, MASSA CHUSETTS

What kinds of things make people happy?

— Being alone sometimes.

— Watching flowers blooming.

— When a kiss comes.

—John Lennon.

What are some things to be sad about?

— *When plants die that I took lots of good care of that I planted all by myself.*

— *When you talk when I'm talking.*

— *If birds didn't come back from the south.*

— *When people have to go to the hospital . . . even mean people.*

— *Running out of coffee.*

What cheers you up when you're down?

—*A lick from my dog.*

—*Oatmeal with chocolate syrup on top.*

—*Fancy dancing.*

—*Wearing underpants on my head.*

—*Eating raisin bread.*

What does it mean when you say to someone, "I love you?"

—*Someone is going to marry you.*

—*It means . . . I don't want to hurt you and I'll always be your friend.*

—*You like the things they do. Some things. Not everything.*

—*I feel you here, in my heart.*

—*I don't remember, but it is very nice.*

What can good friends do for each other?

— *Read stories to each other and sit in each other's laps.*

— *If you have trouble counting, your friend can count for you.*

— *Hold hands and dance.*

— *Be there.*

What's the best way to make a new friend?

— *Say, "Want to be my friend today, please?"*

— *Share dinosaur toys and go for a walk.*

— *Smile.*

Should you always tell the truth? If so, why?

— *Because grownups have special eyes to see everywhere . . . they can see what kids do when they're not looking.*

— *Yes . . . your friends will always tell on you.*

— *I don't know. But if I did, I'd tell you.*

What are examples of big and little lies?

—*Big Lie: Lying to your friends.*
Little Lie: Lying to a teacher.

—*Big Lie: You broke something in a museum*
and said it came to life and just tumbled
out by itself.
Little Lie: Say, "There's a donkey behind
you," when there isn't.

—*There are no little lies. They're all big.*

Do all grownups tell the truth all the time?

— *No. But I'm just guessing.*

— *No, because sometimes they don't want to get in trouble.*

— *No, because sometimes I watch them and listen and sometimes I know they told a little lie.*

What are manners?

—*A different way to say "rules."*

—*You don't say "nah-nah-nah" when you chase someone at tag.*

—*They're so Mom can be alone in the bathroom.*

Why do people wear clothes, even in the summer?

—*So you won't get arrested.*

—*Because they don't want people to see their private parts and belly buttons. People may laugh at them.*

—*Just in case it gets windy.*

What is patience and why is it important?

—*Because if you get in front, then another person could come and get in front of you, and another person in front of him, and then no one will be in front.*

—*It means not saying, "Is it time, is it time, is it time?"*

—*It means don't keep on wanting something. I got no idea why it's so important to grownups.*

What should you do when you feel like hitting someone?

—*Hit a chair. If you hit people you have to sit down in a chair.*

—*Just hit them very lightly so it won't hurt.*

—*Squeeze your brain.*

—*Ask them if they want to be hit.*

What is war?

— *Oh, that's a tough one. When two generals get very angry and they don't want to be friends and they have a lot of men and guns and they fight at people and stuff and people get killed. That's the sad part. The best part is when they make friends again. You see, the good guys and bad guys are fighting, but they're bad guys to each other. So we don't know who is the good guy or the bad guy.*

Why do countries fight wars?

— *They don't know about sharing.*

— *Because they don't like cats and think the other country has cats.*

— *Because they don't stop to think there are other ways to solve problems.*

What could people do instead of fighting wars?

—*Just say "no," because you don't want friends to die.*

—*Make friendships. I won't get into your country if you won't get into my country.*

—*Marry each other.*

—*Spend time with their families.*

What does the president of our country do?

— *Is he like God?*

— *He makes laws, arrests people, and talks on TV.*

— *Orders everybody around. And writes the Declaration of Independence.*

— *He gets a day off whenever he wants because he's in charge.*

— *He tells people to stop at red lights . . . he tells us to put on our seat belts when we drive in the car, and lock the door when we leave the house.*

Should the president always tell the truth and keep his promises?

— *Yes; if he doesn't, he'll get fired.*

— *Yes, if he wants to be a boss.*

— *No, he doesn't have to. But if he was a kid, he would.*

If you were the president of our country, what's the most important rule you'd make?

— *No one would be allowed outside when it's slippery.*

— *No divorce allowed.*

— *Treat plants nicely.*

— *The rich would have to give money to the poor, and at the bank only the poor people could take out money if they really need it. And they don't have to give it back.*

What does the vice president do?

— *He's the assistant president. He does stuff like guard the White House if the president's out.*

— *He golfs.*

— *Helps the president clean up.*

— *Is he some kind of tool?*

Could a woman be president or vice president?

—*Yes, because it wouldn't be fair if only boys were able to.*

—*No, because a woman isn't strong enough to either have a sword to kill someone who did something wrong or to beat them up.*

—*Yes. A girl could be president, because girls are smarter and aren't always fighting and pushing.*

Who has more fun—girls or boys?

— *Girls, 'cause girls like kisses more than boys do.*

— *Boys, because they mind more of their own business.*

Who has more fun—grownups or kids?

—A kid, because you can go up higher on the swing.

— Grownups, because you can stay up as late as you want and plug things in.

— Grownups . . . you can wear high heels.

Why do some men lose their hair as they grow up?

— *They get short short short short haircuts.*

— *Their mommies cut it off.*

— *It must have blown away.*

— *I guess a barber shop cut it all off and their hair died.*

— *When they go skiing . . . it gets frozen and cracks off.*

— *They forgot to put their hair seeds in.*

Why do grownups work?

— *So they don't get bored.*

— *It's something to do after they eat breakfast.*

— *They signed up.*

— *Because they're so big they can't go to school.*

— *To make milk money.*

— *So they can ride the bus.*

If someone was working too hard or upset about work, what would you say?

— *Get a grip.*

— *Stop work, go outside, and take a long walk in a meadow.*

— *Take a tub.*

— *Don't think about it now . . . see how it goes the next day.*

What do grownups do after they put their children to bed?

— *Order pizza.*

— *Play with the toys.*

— *Stuff we'd like to do.*

— *Mom reads Dad a story.*

What are dreams?

— *Going someplace else when you're sleeping.*

— *They're thoughts. If you're worried or scared during the day, they get scrambled up like a jigsaw puzzle. Then they get mixed together at night, and instead of the thought, it becomes a bad dream.*

— *Dreams come out of a big pipe. Bad dreams come from the top part of the pipe, happy dreams from the bottom, and sad dreams from the left side.*

— *We have to have imagination, don't we?*

Who is the Tooth Fairy?

— *The Tooth Fairy is married to the Sandman. They both work at night. First the Sandman sprinkles sand in the children's eyes so they sleep and can't see his wife. Then the Tooth Fairy comes. She is very small and thin, like flat, so she can slip between the pillows. She has a pocket book for money and a basket for teeth. She has sparkly wings and wears a pink skirt. I saw her when Larissa's tooth fell out. I pretended to be asleep, but I was peeking.*

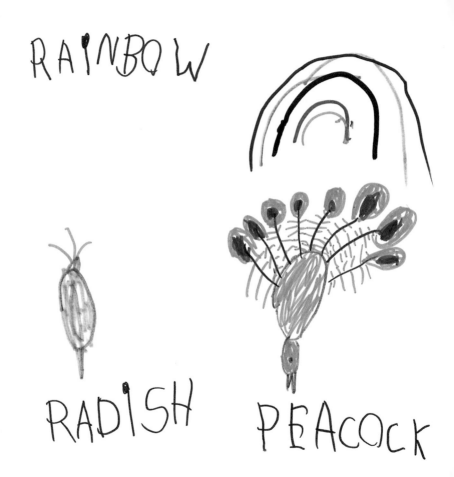

RAINBOW

RADISH

PEACOCK

Besides people, what other things are beautiful?

— *Peacocks and radishes. Radishes are pretty dark pink and have green.*

— *Pink flamingoes.*

— *My guinea pig.*

What makes rainbows?

— *There is a beautiful woman who has a string made of beautiful colors. And when she flies she hooks it onto the sky.*

— *Beautiful pencils.*

— *The rainbow fairy.*

— *Pieces of the sunset.*

Why is the sky blue?

— *God used a blue crayon.*

— *The sky was the first thing made and everything was blue back then.*

— *Blue raindrops.*

— *Because if the sky was white you wouldn't be able to see the clouds.*

— *It's God's favorite color.*

What do you think the "big bang" was like?

—*Like somebody stomping.*

—*It must have been when the dinosaurs were fighting.*

— *"Boom!"*

—*It gave everyone a very bad headache.*

What really happened to the dinosaurs?

— *They didn't eat the right stuff.*

— *They died and their bones fell out, then guys brought them with trucks to the museum.*

— *A giant dinosaur chased all the others up a tree and ate them. Then he had no more food and he died.*

— *They just didn't feel like existing any more.*

Do you think the dinosaurs may come back someday?

— No. They're all at the museum.

— No. They are extinct and they are smelly and won't be back until the humans are gone.

— Yes. They'll be here on Friday, in Natick.

What do cats and dogs think about when they're alone?

— *Cat food. And dog food.*

— *Their relatives.*

— *"Man, where is everybody?"*

What is the "greenhouse effect"?

—*It's like a big compost pile. Plants go there to get green.*

—*I only know about the White House. The president lives in the White House. I guess the vice president lives in the Green House.*

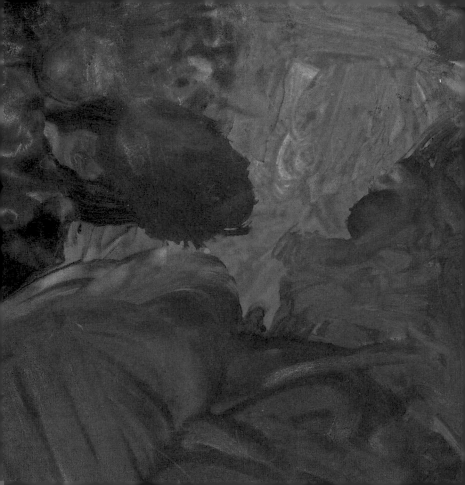

What is the "ozone hole"?

—*It's a place for bad people. The bad guys will come out and get fire to put in the hole and then the hole will get bigger. And then they can all go in at one time. Then it closes into a little hole and they can't get out.*

Do you think there are people on other planets?

— *Yes. The colors and stripes on the planets mean there are houses.*

— *Yes . . . sometimes they look like people in my class.*

— *Yes. I am one.*

Where were you before you were born?

—*In the other room.*

—*I was just a wish.*

—*In mommy's tummy. Before that I was in God's stomach.*

—*Grandma's house.*

—*Indiana.*

GOD

If you could ask God one question, what would it be?

— *Why are you here?*

— *Where do you sleep?*

— *How did you make yourself?*

— *How old are you?*

— *Do you have any food up there so I can eat after I die?*

— *How's grandpop doing?*

What are some impossible things?

—*You could never be eaten by a microwave.*

—*For a whale to ride the bus.*

—*Nobody could balance on the top of a door because they'd get squished.*

Is there any impossible thing you wish could happen?

— *To see God.*

— *Let everybody be happy.*

— *The whole wide world didn't fight and we didn't have nightmares and we didn't have cavities.*

KIDS' ANSWERS TO LIFE'S BIG QUESTIONS

Special thanks are in order to the following children, who provided answers and/or artwork for the questions indicated.

WHAT KINDS OF THINGS MAKE PEOPLE HAPPY? Robby Bishop;
 Timothy Sepkoski St. Clair; Jessica Lord; David Toropov. *ART:* Anna
 Norcross.

WHAT ARE SOME THINGS TO BE SAD ABOUT? Anna Norcross;
 Nicholas Ward; Timothy Sepkoski St. Clair; Elizabeth Straus; Emily
 Smith. *ART:* Jacob Sagrans.

WHAT CHEERS YOU UP WHEN YOU'RE DOWN? Ciara Lydon;
 Suzanne Swann; Erica Siwila-Sackman; Noah Bennett; Emily Smith.
 ART: Erica Siwila-Sackman.

WHAT DOES IT MEAN WHEN YOU SAY TO SOMEONE, "I LOVE
 YOU?" Maggie Wilson; Rebecca Chauncey Thal; Anna Norcross;
 Brian Douglas; Andrew Luehring. *ART:* Caitlin Marshall.

WHAT CAN GOOD FRIENDS DO FOR EACH OTHER? Cameron Brett;
 Deena Alex; Mor Kushilevitz; Mark Buckley. *ART:* Caitlin Marshall.

WHAT'S THE BEST WAY TO MAKE A NEW FRIEND? Molly
 Dunn-Hardy; Geoff Fraser; Keith Warren. *ART:* Kobi Ernstoff.

SHOULD YOU ALWAYS TELL THE TRUTH? IF SO, WHY? David
 Maltzan; Leigh Ann Van Scoy; Anna Leigh Coleman. *ART:* Amy Seigal.

WHAT ARE EXAMPLES OF BIG AND LITTLE LIES? Matt
 Dilts-Williams; Nathaniel Seelen; Felishia Mangla. *ART:* Caitlin
 Marshall.

DO ALL GROWNUPS TELL THE TRUTH ALL THE TIME? Peter Beyel;
 Robby Bishop; Phillip deRochemont. *ART:* Simon Moody.

KIDS' ANSWERS TO LIFE'S BIG QUESTIONS

WHAT ARE MANNERS? Zachary Miller; Jeremy Finch; Aurora Cremer. *ART:* Grace Laubacher.

WHY DO PEOPLE WEAR CLOTHES, EVEN IN THE SUMMER? Phillip deRochemont; Aaron Lefkowitz; Benjamin Eisen. *ART:* Jessica Lord.

WHAT IS PATIENCE AND WHY IS IT IMPORTANT? Thomas Wickersham; Christopher Migner; David Maltzan. *ART:* Donna Cleri.

WHAT SHOULD YOU DO WHEN YOU FEEL LIKE HITTING SOMEONE? Will Kalish; Zachary Miller; Andrew Luehring; Noah Bennett. *ART:* Erica Siwila-Sackman.

WHAT IS WAR? Christopher Pergola. *ART:* Rachel Freierman.

WHY DO COUNTRIES FIGHT WARS? Kobi Ernstoff; Hilary Friedman; Rebecca Chauncey Thal. *ART:* Grace Laubacher.

WHAT COULD PEOPLE DO INSTEAD OF FIGHTING WARS? Ryan Murphy; Rachele Conley; Leigh Ann Van Scoy; Julia Mellin. *ART:* Zoe Ripple.

WHAT DOES THE PRESIDENT OF OUR COUNTRY DO? Stephanie Bambury; Mark Buckley; Nathaniel Seelen; Peter Beyel; Emily Smith. *ART:* Grace Laubacher.

SHOULD THE PRESIDENT ALWAYS TELL THE TRUTH AND KEEP HIS PROMISES? Eric Beck; Stephanie Bambury; Robby Bishop. *ART:* Grace Laubacher.

IF YOU WERE THE PRESIDENT OF OUR COUNTRY, WHAT'S THE MOST IMPORTANT RULE YOU'D MAKE? Rebecca Chauncey Thal; Kayla Stanley; Kayla Stanley; Lacey Benedict. *ART:* Zoe Ripple.

WHAT DOES THE VICE PRESIDENT DO? Eric Beck; Katie Fryer; David Horowitz; Sarah Johnson. *ART:* Rachel Freierman.

COULD A WOMAN BE PRESIDENT OR VICE PRESIDENT? Julia Mellin; Kobi Ernstoff; Lacey Benedict. *ART:* Lacey Benedict.

KIDS' ANSWERS TO LIFE'S BIG QUESTIONS

WHO HAS MORE FUN—GIRLS OR BOYS? Anna Norcross; Lee Thompson. *ART:* Rachel Freierman.

WHO HAS MORE FUN—GROWNUPS OR KIDS? Anna Leigh Coleman; Timothy Sepkoski St. Clair; Ainsley Mallows. *ART:* Rachel Freierman.

WHY DO SOME MEN LOSE THEIR HAIR AS THEY GROW UP? Anna Leigh Coleman; Will Kalish; David Maltzan; Andrew Luehring; Timmy Glanville; Timothy Sepkoski St. Clair. *ART:* David Maltzan.

WHY DO GROWNUPS WORK? Sander Randall; Anna Leigh Coleman; Mark Buckley; Jessica Lord; Peter Beyel; Paige Pollom. *ART:* Grace Laubacher.

IF SOMEONE WAS WORKING TOO HARD OR UPSET ABOUT WORK, WHAT WOULD YOU SAY? Andrew Luehring; Noah Bennett; Grace Laubacher; Mark Buckley. *ART:* Donna Cleri.

WHAT DO GROWNUPS DO AFTER THEY PUT THEIR CHILDREN TO SLEEP? Patrick Hyland; Myles Lynch; Kobi Ernstoff; Maggie Wilson. *ART:* Caitlin Marshall.

WHAT ARE DREAMS? Anna Leigh Coleman; Kobi Ernstoff; Benjamin Eisen; Deena Alex. *ART:* Mor Kushilevitz.

WHO IS THE TOOTH FAIRY? Lacey Benedict. *ART:* Lacey Benedict.

BESIDES PEOPLE, WHAT OTHER THINGS ARE BEAUTIFUL? Lacey Benedict; Kobi Ernstoff; Robby Bishop. *ART:* Lacey Benedict.

WHAT MAKES RAINBOWS? Lucas Coleman; Will Kalish; Keith Warren; Benjamin Eisen. *ART:* Samantha Sacco.

WHY IS THE SKY BLUE? Anna Leigh Coleman; Lucas Coleman; Anna Norcross; Kobi Ernstoff; Suzanne Swann. *ART:* Donna Cleri.

WHAT DO YOU THINK THE "BIG BANG" WAS LIKE? Deena Alex; Stephanie Bambury; Molly Dunn-Hardy; Noah Bennett. *ART:* Noah Bennett.

KIDS' ANSWERS TO LIFE'S BIG QUESTIONS

WHAT REALLY HAPPENED TO THE DINOSAURS? Amy Seigal; Andrew Luehring; Noah Bennett; Rebecca Chauncey Thal. *ART:* Lacey Benedict.

DO YOU THINK THE DINOSAURS MAY COME BACK SOMEDAY? Myles Lynch; Benjamin Sattin; Joseph Dumas. *ART:* Peter Beyel.

WHAT DO CATS AND DOGS THINK ABOUT WHEN THEY'RE ALONE? Simon Moody; Rebecca Chauncey Thal; Kayla Stanley. *ART:* Grace Laubacher.

WHAT IS THE "GREENHOUSE EFFECT"? Noah Bennett; Lacey Benedict. *ART:* Myles Lynch.

WHAT IS THE "OZONE HOLE"? Jessica Lord. *ART:* Andrew Aylward.

DO YOU THINK THERE ARE PEOPLE ON OTHER PLANETS? Benjamin Sattin; Amy Seigal; Timothy Sepkoski St. Clair. *ART:* Lucas Coleman.

WHERE WERE YOU BEFORE YOU WERE BORN? Noah Bennett; Rebecca Chauncey Thal; Sarah Johnson; Jessica Lord; Will Kalish. *ART:* Grace Laubacher.

IF YOU COULD ASK GOD ONE QUESTION, WHAT WOULD IT BE? Cameron Gibbins; Katie Fryer; Lucas Coleman; Anna Leigh Coleman; Andrew Luehring; Eric Beck. *ART:* Lacey Benedict.

WHAT ARE SOME IMPOSSIBLE THINGS? Kayla Stanley; Noah Bennett; Joseph Dumas. *ART:* Jessica Lord.

IS THERE ANY IMPOSSIBLE THING YOU WISH COULD HAPPEN? Kobi Ernstoff; Lacey Benedict; Elizabeth Straus. *ART:* Caitlin Marshall.

About the Authors

STEVE BENNETT is a full-time author who has written more than 35 books on topics ranging from business and computing to environmental issues and parenting. Most recently, he and his wife, Ruth, co-authored the best-selling *365 TV-Free Activities You Can Do with Your Child* (Bob Adams, Inc.).

RUTH LOETTERLE BENNETT is a landscape architect who has designed parks, playgrounds, and other public places in a number of cities in the United States. She co-wrote and illustrated the couple's TV-free activity book.

An Invitation

If your children have answers to life's big questions that you would like to share with the Bennetts, you can write them at P.O. Box 1646, Harvard Square Station, Cambridge, MA 02238.